LIGHT THAT
SPLITS THE DARK

LIGHT
that Splits
the DARK

THE SOLITUDE PAPERS II
EDITED BY PAUL ELMO KEENAN

PUBLISHERS PLACE

Distributed to the trade by
Cumberland House Publishing
431 Harding Industrial Drive
Nashville, Tennessee 37211

First Edition • First Printing
Printed in Canada

Library of Congress Catalog Number: 2001095203
ISBN: 0-9676051-4-8

Project Coordination: John Patrick Grace, Ph.D., and Amanda Ballard
Book and Cover Design, Photography: Mark S. Phillips

Publishers Place, Inc.
945 Fourth Avenue, Suite 200A
Huntington, WV 25701
publish@cloh.net

www.publishersplace.org

DEDICATION

Verizon employees across West Virginia
congratulate the rising generation of young writers
who made this collection possible.
Their remarkably thoughtful works of art
represent them, their families and schools, and our state
in the highest manner.

Publication of this work was made possible
by a grant from Verizon Foundation

FOREWORD

When Dr. Grace first gave me *River Fog Rising* to read and told me the formula that went into the writing of its essays, I had only one thought: "Why couldn't someone have done something like this for me when I was 17?" I read the students' reflections and saw the enlightenment they gained from the experience. They saw for the first time things they had taken for granted their whole lives. Clearly, they realized the things they had understood to be so important were not that consequential when they put themselves in the perspective of the greatness surrounding them.

I could read the process of the assignment in their words: the reading and discussion of Anne Morrow Lindbergh's book, *Gift from the Sea*, followed by a list of questions the students were given to ponder:

> *Who am I?*
> *What is my life all about?*
> *Where am I in relation to those who came*
>   *before me and lived in this place?*
> *Who am I to those who will come after me?*
> *What will my life be like five years from now? Ten?*
> *What kind of contributions can I make that will*
>   *make a difference?*

After this the students were asked to envision themselves looking back over their lives from the point of their deaths. Lastly, they spent an hour of solitude in nature with a pen and notebook to record their thoughts.

Their words proved they had read the material, listened

to the instructions, and pondered what was required. Each student was successful in preparing for the assignment before getting close to nature or putting pen to page. The words they produced were testimony to the level of attention they had given the process.

The same is true for *Light That Splits the Dark*, in which we followed the same curriculum, adding Henry David Thoreau's *Walden*, Annie Dillard's *Pilgrim at Tinker's Creek*, and *River Fog Rising* as possible substitutions for the Lindbergh book.

The teachers, of whom I have formulated good and positive impressions through our correspondences, were all passionate about the project. The students felt this passion and followed it. The words they gave us to work with were filled with hope, awareness, love, determination, and all of those other things that we want to fill out students' words. In these days after Columbine, they ask us some of the questions they have on their minds. If we read their words, and listen to what they are saying, we might be able to give them some answers.

Aside from the obvious benefits of respect for nature, solitude, and reflection, I hope the students take from this experience an awareness of the accessibility of writing's release. Would-be writers are so often removed from the craft because they don't think they write well or don't think they have something to say. I hope these students learned this is not true. I hope they saw how easily the words came once a teacher gave them the questions, provided them with the reading, put them in the setting, and stuck pens in their hands. If they did, they will carry this experience with them and know that writing is not that difficult when you get passed the negative thoughts about how to do it.

These students have only one more step to take to become writers — if they are not already; they have to become the teachers. They have to ask the questions, find the books, perfect the settings, and grab the pens. And they know it's not that hard.

I would like to thank each of them for making this possible. We could have presented the project and the teachers could have taught it, but it never would have happened if the students didn't go out and create it. I would also like to thank Sara Welch from Buffalo High School, Fay Stump from Weir High School, Melissa Bannister at Parkersburg South High School, Gregory Rickard at Wahama High School, and Patricia Jones at Van High School for taking time away from regular their lesson plans for *Light That Splits the Dark*. I would like to thank my family for being my support in all endeavors. Lastly, I would like to thank Dr. John Patrick Grace. Nobody gave me this assignment when I was 17, but he gave it to me later and allowed me to share it with others. I guess anytime is a good time to learn a worthwhile process.

— *Paul Elmo Keenan*

NIGHT LIGHT

It's a bright source of light that splits the dark.
Its glow, shape and grace are seen by all.
It's there in winter, spring, summer and fall.
In the dark of night it shows all a spark.

We did make a point to walk upon it.
We all look up at it when passing by.
That shiny thing's the biggest in our sky.
We wanted to know how our nights kept lit.

Its glow—the sign that represents our night.
A full one!—beautiful, and a wondrous sight.
Its size makes other night objects little.
It looks strong but in ways kind of brittle.

In the daytime hours night's time is done,
That glowing orb? The moon, not the sun.

—*Kevin Chattin*

Originally published in *River Fog Rising: The Solitude Papers*,
Publishers Place, Inc., 1996.

ERIC ALATIS
Weir High School

As I observe my surroundings, I ask, "Who am I?" This question isn't as simple as it sounds. First, I think of myself as a student. I think I will always be a student, even after I've graduated from high school and college. I mean that I will always be learning. I am learning how to live my life the way I want. My classmates, presumably, are learning something similar. I hope to learn as much as I can in my life, so I can better understand why we are here. Everyone has his or her own opinion of why we are here, but no one knows for sure. I think I am here to make the most of my life. I believe I'm doing a fair job.

I think I will be nervous five years from now, as I will be past my senior year of high school and preparing to enter the "real world." I have always had my parents to make sure I do everything right. Eventually, I will have to show someone else right from wrong. I don't know how I will handle this. I will be ready some day, I think, and will be able to teach my own children right from wrong. This will help them lead successful lives.

As I am leaving my spot in the woods, I try to figure out what my surroundings make me think of. The trees and wooded area make me think of primitive times when people didn't have the luxuries we now have. They make me more thankful for what I do have.

BRETT ALLEN
Weir High School

Saturday, I was in a terrible car accident. We were driving down Lick Run Road, and an approaching vehicle was in our lane. Avoiding this car, our vehicle flipped and rolled into King's Creek. We are fortunate to be alive, and today I am very reflective.

Who am I? I am my mother's only child. Her hopes, dreams, and life are wrapped into me. Seeing her weep in my arms that day was too much. It's safe to say that my life is always about my parents. My friends matter too, but my parents are the reason I exist. They were the first people I saw after the accident.

I was given a second chance. Therefore, I think I must have some purpose in life. While I could have died that day, I was fortunate enough to come out with only a few scratches. Now I am thankful for my friends and their concerns. It doesn't matter where I'll be in five or ten years. As long as I'm alive and happy, I can ask for nothing more.

Throughout the chaos, I was mostly concerned for David-James. While I knew I was all right, I wasn't sure about him, and I was scared. I knew that all I could do was be there with him. As long as he wasn't alone, I felt I was making a difference.

So, as I sit here and watch the water trickle beneath my feet, I realize that we don't have all the time in the world. We take the simple things for granted, but, as I look around today, I am taking everything in.

DANIELLE ARIA

Weir High School

I could sit in this spot, on this rock, forever. It's so peaceful and untouched by human hands. My father used to bring me to this place when I was younger. It seemed like it took hours to get here; it only takes a few minutes. Fall has just begun and the scenery out here is so beautiful; the sky is so clear; the multicolored leaves move in the crisp breeze.

I sit here, alone, surrounded by nature. My mind moves in a million directions. Soon I am going to college, and soon after that, I hope to begin a family. As for now, I am trying to work on being a better person. I know I now have a better outlook on life than I did a few months ago. I try to live life to the fullest by having as much fun as possible. They say high school is the best time of your life, and I plan to make that statement come true. My friends are so important to me. In two years, we are going to go our separate ways. It will hurt me when that time comes, but I'm not going to make myself miserable thinking about it.

As I take my last look at this spot, I feel more refreshed than I did when I came to this rock an hour ago.

3

MICHELLE BEITZEL

Parkersburg South High School

I keep saying to myself: "It doesn't matter what little choices I make today. They won't affect the rest of my life." The truth is, those little choices are my life. I'm living now. If I am embarrassed, I reassure myself by saying that it isn't going to change my life if I don't answer a question in class or talk out an argument with my mother.

I don't think it will be the major events of my life that I will remember as I approach my death. I think it will be the little things that happened, like the way my mother told me she loved me after we had resolved an argument, or the feeling I got when I overcame my shyness and answered a question in class. Life is every little choice we make; those choices are what we live for.

4

ALISHA BLANKENSHIP
Weir High School

I am at my special spot on King's Creek, separated from the world by a barrier of enormous, continuously aging trees. Boulders are under and all around me. I hear the trickling stream. I feel the icy breeze blowing into my face. The stream travels into a waterfall. Across from the waterfall, another stream drips into this stream, causing a parade of ripples. Does each droplet have a purpose? Do they show how there is a good or bad point to the meaning of life? Are the ripples designed to show the repetition of life? To me, these ripples represent the changes in one's everyday life. The first ripple represents a child being born. The next few represent the child's growing and progressing. The last ripple, fading, represents the end of one's life. I believe all things in my special spot show how no person or creature on earth stays the same indefinitely.

My life will be different in five years because I will have a job, family, and responsibilities. It will be even more different in ten years. I believe this because I think it will happen the way I want if I believe it will. I believe a person begins to die the second he or she is born, and we should all live life to the fullest according to our hearts. I will try to help the next generation understand how one must live one's life fully before death arrives, or never truly have a life at all.

DOUGLAS WINWOOD

Weir High School

Nature Brings Reflection

Trees are families,
Some big and some small.
The fallen leaves are family members,
Gone but not forgotten.

Who am I?
I am a young man put on this earth to bring joy and love
To those who care about me.
Intelligence, humor, and thoughtfulness
Are a few of the qualities I possess.
I am a helpful person
With aspirations of becoming a doctor.
I am a son striving to make his parents proud,
A grandson trying to fulfill his grandparents needs,
A nephew there to help out whenever possible,
A cousin being a role model for those younger than me.
I am a friend who is there to listen.
I am me.

Time is constant.
It will not stop for anyone.
It's hard to believe how much time has already passed in my life.
Soon, I will be a college student.
My hope is to meet someone special and start a family of my own.
I look forward to fatherhood.

I look forward to hearing my children call me "Daddy" and
        tucking them in at night.
I will raise them with unconditional love and endless protection,
The way my parents raised me.

I like how the sun's beams pierce the clouds.
They remind me of spotlights, with each person having their own.
I also like the sunsets when the sky is painted different colors.
My favorite is daybreak blue streaked with fiery crimson flames.
The clouds remind me of the ocean's waves,
Continually in motion and always changing shape.

Nature has a soothing calm to it.
It's a healer for the inner soul.
It is our most precious resource.

7

REX BOGGESS

Weir High School

The early morning sunlight rains through the trees. The golden light reflects off the dewdrops. The scarlet and brown leaves fall to the ground. The sun's rays reflect off of their beauty. It is in this instance that they are at their most beautiful – not when they are green and still connected to the tree, or when they are brown and lying on the ground. They have lived up to this most spectacular moment, when they flutter freely into the wind. They are disconnected from the rest of the community. Their colors are their personalities. This is the stage of life that I'm in right now. I am an individual with beliefs and possibilities different from any other. Without my individuality, I would be just another brown leaf to be walked upon by passers-by.

A chipmunk watches from the bough of a tree, planning his daily routine. He will gather food for the winter months that lay ahead. My life resembles that of the chipmunk. I go to school every day and return home seeking rest. Instead, I find more work to do.

The grass upon which I sit is the same grass that was here for the generations that came before me. I am made of all of my ancestors, and my ancestors to come will be made in part by me.

I am rich, much like the soil that feeds the grass. Not wealthy, but wealthy of mind, and I will continue to contribute my mind to society in the hope that it will help everyone's lives be better.

AMBER CAIN

Parkersburg South High School

I wonder when I say my prayer and go to bed each night if my eyes will ever open again. Even though I am a Christian and Jesus's blood covers me, I am terrified of dying. No one wants to die, but dying is my biggest fear. In the world today prophecies are coming true, announcing to us that Christ's coming is getting closer. What if I'm not ready? Will I stand before God and hear Him say, "Well done. Enter in, my good and faithful servant." Or will he say, "Depart from Me, ye worker of iniquity; I knew you not."

The spiritual battles that are going on in the world are very real, and sometimes I do get scared. Maybe it isn't really death that scares me, but the unknown.

TINA CAIN
Parkersburg South High School

I often wonder why I was born at the time and place, and to whom, I was. I wonder if I'll ever truly understand myself. I wonder what people think of me.

When I look at my life, I'm thankful for what I've got. However, when I look at the world, I think we could accomplish more. In this light, looking around, I am glad I was born where and when, and to whom, I was, whether I understand it or not.

APRIL COEN
Weir High School

T he first sounds I hear while sitting here are the chirping of thousands of birds and insects. It is like another world. These sounds remind me of people talking to each other. No two sounds are alike; each animal and insect has its own distinct sound, just as we do. I would never have thought there would be so much noise out here! Being here, I realize there is nowhere one could go for complete silence because there is always something making noise. Often, we just don't take time to listen.

Looking at the park where I used to play, I can see how much it has changed. Just like it has changed over time, so have I. Change occurs no matter how much we wish it wouldn't. As I sit here, I think of how much my life will be changing in two years. Next year, my senior year, will be my last living here. After I graduate, I will go to college away from everyone and everything I am familiar with. A feeling of sadness comes over me when I think of leaving my family, friends and the only house in which I've ever lived. On the other hand, I have a feeling of anticipation for what lies ahead. Going to college, I will meet new people and see new places and things. I will also learn to live on my own and take care of myself while working to achieve my goals. Five years from now, I hope to be out of college and entering law school. I know there is a lot of work ahead of me, but I am always ready for a challenge.

What contributions of mine will make a difference? What is my life all about? I can't answer these questions because I never really thought about them before right now. I do think God has a plan for everyone. However, I believe it is up to each person to work hard toward achieving their goals.

MICHAEL DALTON

Weir High School

I am in the woods behind my grandmother's house. I am on a stump, on a little hill, watching a trickling stream. I think of how fall is my favorite time of year and how beautiful it is. A strong wind blows and a sea of leaves of all sizes and colors floats to the ground. I see a small chipmunk hurry past me and think I would like to trade places with him. He could go to school, work, and football practice for me and I could just enjoy life in this quiet and wonderful place.

How differently we think of this land than people did 300 years ago. This land once meant survival for the settlers and Native Americans. It provided their food and shelter. If they couldn't have hunted here, they probably would have died of starvation. To many of today's people this place is just somewhere to dump their trash. As I walk along and enjoy the beautiful scenery, I become upset when I see a bathroom sink in the creek, an old tire on the hillside, and empty beer cans on the trail. I don't understand how anyone can throw his or her garbage away in such a beautiful place. People before me cherished the land. People now do not see all that it holds.

MIKE DORSCH
Weir High School

As I sit here by the creek behind my house, I realize how similar I am to it. Being but a trickle, this small stream has left an indention in the earth. People go through life as small individuals, yet each will leave an impression affecting generations long after. I am nothing more than an individual but my life will make a difference in the future.

I badly want to get rid of the hate and violence that our society seems to breed. Even though wishing for world peace may be a bit lofty, I hope to help those afflicted by problems resulting from hate and violence.

Life is like the water in this creek, sometimes rushing by and sometimes trickling along. A rock is like a strong person in that it stands strong and resilient against what life throws at it; sometimes, the rush of the water picks it up and pieces are broken off. At other times, it rests in the stillness and serenity of a pool. Currently, I am like the rock that flows in the rush of the water. My life speeds by, and I wonder at times why I put up with it. Then, I realize that I will eventually reach that serene point in my life. I know this busy time will be worth it when I finally achieve a state of peace, so I work with my all.

There are many people with problems in the world, and after high school I hope to go to college and earn a Ph.D. in Psychiatry so I can help to improve our society's living conditions. If I can help a few people, I believe my life will be complete. I will have left my mark.

When it all boils down, I am a boy growing and learning every day, and trying hard to be the person I want to be. Later in life, I will still be that same boy, experiencing new things that will continue to shape me. Just as the erosion caused by the creek shapes the rock, I will be shaped constantly until death.

Walking back to my house after this experience, I am faced with a sight that astonishes me. A tree that always seemed so old and strong to me when I was a child is now dead. It makes me realize that I, like the tree, will not live forever. So, until my time to die comes, I am going to enjoy every day and every gift that God offers me.

AMANDA DUTTINE

Buffalo High School

The different colors of grass on the field are like the different decisions of my life. The brown ones are the decisions that have fizzled out and are now forgotten. The bright green ones are the decisions that are still sparkling, and have brought something good to my life. These represent the times when I have chosen correctly. Both the pale and the dark green ones represent those decisions when I did not take enough time to think and when I made the wrong choice.

I hope to have a life that is like an unblemished, bright green field.

DIANE ELLIOT
Weir High School

As I sit here, a falling leaf reminds me nothing is permanent. Every thing has an end. The leaf's end makes me wonder how my life will end. I'm too young to die now. I haven't discovered myself yet. I am a small piece of a big puzzle as that leaf was a small part of that tree. Will I become a bigger, more important piece in time? Am I even needed to complete the puzzle? Even though I know I should just live the life I have today, I can't stop worrying about the future. I need to sit back and relax. I need to enjoy nature.

I have now moved from my original spot. I walk up the path to the springs. Along the way I watch the creek and am reminded of how pretty the world is in the fall. I am now sitting on a bridge in front of the cliffs. The sound of the water is so calming. I hear a bird in flight and wonder where it is going. Is it going to find food for its young? I can't wait until I can feed my babies. I can't wait to see them grow. By being a good mother I hope to help my children become good parents. I think being a parent is the most important job there is. Parents help create people's behavior, and bad parenting can possibly help produce a killer or an abuser. I think there would be fewer murders if there were more good parents.

The sounds around me have gotten louder as more birds join the first one. All people would realize how beautiful nature is if they would just give it a little time. I won't let this be my last time out here.

NATALIE FAULK
Wahama High School

I wonder if the fog that will settle around us in five or ten years will look the same as this fog, and if I'll even remember this. Is it possible that I will never see some of my friends again after this year is over? These thoughts run through my mind most waking moments. My friends have been with me for most of my life. What will I do without them? I don't exactly know, but I guess that's how life is.

These strong trees are about the only stable thing around here. People come and go, leaving trails of laughter and tears. Buildings age with every gust of wind and leave behind only the remnant of something that once stood proud. I think aging is one of life's cruel qualities. Just to know that each passing moment sees your life knocked down a notch is scary.

As the leaves change color in the morning's mist, I find a sense of serenity. Feeling unreachable, I sit and reflect. Life is a mystery with no set plan or course. Everything is a challenge with perfection being the biggest one of all. It is the unattainable dream. My stay in solitude is coming to an end, and I will leave amid these thoughts. I think I have found that living life to one's own expectations is the key to success. We should not change ourselves despite what others think.

Sitting here and reflecting upon myself has cleared my mind. Stress and frustration have been lifted, leaving only me, my own person.

HILLARY FIELDS
Wahama High School

As the wind blows gently through the trees, tiny particles of dandelions scatter in every direction. They do not know where they are going, but simply trust God that they will land in a place good enough to plant their seeds and flourish. In a way, I am a dandelion. Upon graduation, I have no idea where the wind will carry me. I will be carried off to a new place to make new friends, start my career and begin a family. I hope I will not forget where I came from, the friends I made – and in some cases, lost – and the lessons I've learned.

I will carry the experience of growing up with me throughout my life and apply it in a tomorrow that waits with countless possibilities. Who knows what direction the wind will be blowing? I can only imagine.

DON FISHER
Weir High School

I think of myself as a pretty good kid. I go to church and always try to do right. I think my parents have raised me to be a good, responsible son. I hope to raise my children the way my parents raised me. They are good to me but discipline me when I need it. I'd like to be that kind of parent. I want my children to be proud of me, and say the same things about me that I now say about my parents. I want them to be raised in a Christian home, with both parents there to support them.

I'd like to get good enough at baseball so I can provide well for my family. I want people to admire the way I live my life. I want my children to grow up with strong relationships with God, and to have good lives.

JEREMY FORTUNE

Parkersburg South High School

I often think about how humanity tries to understand its place in the universe. This thought resembles the question, "What is the meaning of life?" Teenagers like myself often ask this question but seldom come up with a suitable answer. I have asked this question many times and believe I have found something very rare, a solution.

It began with a search for myself, trying to discern what in my life was truth and what was a lie. Disappointingly, I found many lies or stories that were created without much thought. Some of the "lies" were simple misunderstandings. I think that no human being truly understands a parable or saying until they are wise enough to create the saying themselves. By the time that this happens, the damage has already been done and the saying that was created to protect oneself is useless.

My life consists of learning. I have an unquenchable thirst for knowledge. I study people's minds and personalities, trying to comprehend how they have lived their lives, and why.

At some point in my search I realized that I had the ability to truly know myself. However, because I had learned so much about my surrounding world, I no longer wished to understand. I was satisfied with what I already knew.

I believe it is virtually impossible for someone to ever know themselves, and that by the time someone does, they don't need to anymore.

LUKE FRAZIER

Parkersburg South High School

What makes me who I am? This question fills me with emotion and thought. It's as if I am analyzing a beautiful piece of art, and I ask myself, "Why is this beautiful?" I could offer a shallow response like, "The color is good," but that's not it. It's the feeling it gives you inside – visually indescribable – which makes it beautiful. At times, we don't realize that these feelings make us who we are.

Music is another component of the tapestry of life for me. Not only a soft melody on the air, but nature's music as well. Music with no set key or pitch – music which cannot be concealed. The music of the wind blowing through the trees, or the sound of a babbling brook combined with the song of a perched bird. This music fills my body and soul. It gives me feelings and emotions that help shape my life and make me the unique individual I am.

JILL GRACIE

Weir High School

It may seem silent out here in the woods, but if you truly listen, you will realize that it's not silence that fills the air, but nature's musical performance. The wind whispers like an audience watching the stage before a play. The birds harmonize and give one another a turn in the spotlight. The trees applaud with their rustling leaves, and the wind whistles its encore.

Right now, I feel as if my life is an ocean constantly in motion. Waves are produced by harsh words in my life as they are by a boat in the ocean. Where the wave begins is where it hurts the most, but the ripples don't feel as if they will ever decrease in pain. However, as the ripples subside, I am soothed and calmed until another ship rolls by.

I take a deep breath and close my eyes. I can feel the heat of the sun upon my back. It is so relaxing to open my eyes and turn my head to see the rays shining through the trees, spreading bands of sunshine on everything.

Now I am lying on the pokey grass, trying to find a comfortable position. I laugh, but what is so funny? If anyone can hear, they must think it absurd. When I calm down, I realize why I love nature so much. It is beautiful, musical, and it will laugh with me, so I don't feel alone or absurd. Laughter is one of the keys to my life, and I can share it with my remembered love — Nature.

DENISE HARMON
Buffalo High School

As I sit and think on this glorious morning, I see a bug: "Does he know where he is going?" "What direction might his life take?" "Will he live for years or just a few days?" "Does he know why he is here and what he is going to do?"

The more I think about the bug, the more I think of myself. Do I know the answers to these questions as regards myself? I sit here thinking about the bug, but what about me? Now that I think of these things I see how much I am like the bug. I don't think either of us knows what's going to happen in our lives. Someday I might know. For now, however, I am going to be like the bug, and wait for whatever life might bring me. Whatever I find, I will think of my bug.

MATT HEIM
Weir High School

I am myself. I am a unique person. I am on the beach at Cedar Point in Sandusky, Ohio. It is 11:00 p.m., and there is a full moon shimmering off Lake Erie. In the distance I hear the faint screams of people on roller coasters. There is no light but the moon. I can barely see the paper. There are no people around me.

Sea gulls are all around me. I wonder if they know I'm here. I can hear, see, and feel the lake's water coming up and touching my feet. It is so nice to be able to sit here and think.

I hope my future is the way I see it: Married with twin daughters, successful, and happy. The sea gulls remind me of humans searching for their destiny.

My life is so busy: work, school, Octaves, band, extra jobs, homework, football games, family, piano lessons, saxophone lessons, Mexico trip, New York trip, band trip, and friends. I feel like there is so much I haven't mentioned. I'm spinning from all the activity and have trouble deciding where to begin sometimes. I think I'm going to have a nervous breakdown if I don't do more of nothing.

I love my friends. I can tell them everything and have fun with them. I love this time. I love being able to stop and think about myself and others.

MATT OWENS
Buffalo High School

I could become as big and stout
as a Redwood tree.
I could become as stubborn
as a Thorn tree.
I could become as old and droopy
as a Weeping Willow.
There are many things I could become
as I grow older.

ALICIA HELGESEN

Weir High School

Who am I? I am joy. I am a river, raging through the rough rapids of life and flowing through the calm of pleasant times. Does this river have a purpose?

I believe one Supreme Being created this river and all of nature. It has been here forever. I, on the other hand, will not be here forever. How many people have sat on this rock and watched the river? How many animals have come here to drink from its water? Will I like this river be important in the future? Will I make a difference? Will generations to come appreciate this river or will they be too caught up in technology to notice it? Why, as time passes, do we seem to ignore nature more and more? Nature is beautiful. Life is beautiful. I want my life to be like nature and give people a sense of peace.

One doesn't realize how cluttered and loud her or his life is until they experience the simplicity and calm of the outdoors. Being here makes me realize that I need to enjoy my life more. I need to slow down, think more and not take things for granted.

When I'm in nature, time stops. Every thing, every part of nature is unified. It is one being. I am part of that being. I am no longer an onlooker. I am no longer outside of nature. I am nature.

MAGGIE HOWARD

Buffalo High School

I think I'm like a piece of old gum. I stick to my goals like this gum sticks to the sole of my shoe. I plan to make something out of my life, and I will stick to my goals until I achieve this.

I can become anything I want. I want to be someone's role model. I want to help people in one way or another. I can make a contribution that makes the world a better place. I would and will do anything possible for others. I will keep working until I reach my goals. If one comes across that is impossible, I'll put it aside and find a new goal.

JEREMIAH JEFFERS

Buffalo High School

My life is like a small tree. It doesn't have any branches and isn't very big yet. The leaves are my thoughts and opinions. They will change throughout the course of my life. The branches are the different activities I am involved in, as well as the roles I play: student, son, and brother. The knots and imperfections are the mistakes of my life. Since my tree is young, it doesn't have a rough, rigid bark.

Just as my tree matures and grows to give the world shade, I hope I will be able to give something to the world – something different and memorable.

ANNA LEISURE

Parkersburg South High School

I am afraid of dying and being remembered as a follower instead of a leader. I am afraid of being remembered as a person who would not show her true colors because it might lead someone to get mad and not like them anymore. I'm afraid of not reaching my goals because I listened to people when they told me I couldn't do this or be that.

There are many things I am afraid of but I know I can handle anything life throws at me as long as I have family and friends to support me along the way.

TARA LEWIS
Buffalo High School

I see myself as a twinkling star in the sky – a star that is hidden during the day or on a cloudy night. It's waiting for the sun to go down or for a cloud to move so that it can come out and show the world its bright, beautiful light. Likewise I am waiting for my chance to make a difference in someone's life, to have one person see me when I come out from behind my cloud and say, "I want to be like her." Not the "me" on the basketball court or at school, but the "me" who is still hiding behind the cloud.

A person cannot get too close to a real star, it will burn or blind them. But what if someone did actually touch a real star, would it die or would it shine brighter? I don't know and maybe the stars don't either. Maybe that is why they only come out on clear, calm nights. Maybe this is the same reason I find it hard to let people get close to me. God made each star special, just like he made me special. I feel really close to God in my own life, and I really want to shine for Him. But I will just wait behind that cloud, waiting for that night, when I can come out and show the world the real me.

MELISSA LITTLE
Buffalo High School

My life is all about family, friends, religion, and school. I would compare my life to a tree because it has many branches. With my family, I play the roles of daughter, big sister, and even mother and father when my mother and father are not around to do so. I have to be strong and encouraging to others around me. There may be fights within my family at times, and I may find myself "falling off," as leaves do in the fall, but I always grow back.

Friends, religion, and school are other branches on the tree of my life, and I have to keep all of these branches and leaves balanced so I don't tip over.

In five years I hope to be like a rose, and blooming in my education.

LEAH LOUBIERE

Parkersburg South High School

Everyday I wake up wondering what my life will be like in the future. Sometimes I am afraid that the goal I set for myself might be too hard to accomplish. I have never been indecisive about what I want to do when I grow up. I want to be an actress. I want to be known and loved, not just for my talent, but for my kindness. I want to be one of those who is always giving to the community.

I dream of a loving relationship and a tight-knit family. When I have kids, I hope to be the mom that everybody loves.

I also hold high expectations for my friends and my family. Each time I sit down to plot out my future, my expectations get higher. My biggest fear is that I might fall short of my goals and not reach the level of happiness I seek.

TONY MACRE

Weir High School

As I sit here in the solitude the woods offer, I get a chance to look back on my life – and also forward. I have such a hectic life that I never get the opportunity to just sit back and think. Having to worry about getting an "A" on an English paper and trying to remember if I have all of my equipment for a game are daily worries.

But being out here, I realize that my life isn't bad at all. My parents take good care of me, and I know that my friends will always be there for me. I am a friend, student, cousin, brother, grandson, and son. Sometimes it becomes difficult to fulfill all of the needs these roles require. Sometimes I need a break from the pressure. That is why I now feel that I should come into the woods more often, just to take the time to reflect on how my life is progressing.

In five years, I believe I will be enrolled in college, gaining an education for a job. I don't believe the future will see me making a large impact on many people. I don't think I'll become a well-known man, but I think I'll become a successful businessman, or something of that nature. I don't know what the future will bring, so I plan to play the roles life offers me. And enjoy the ride.

VINCE MAGNONE
Weir High School

A s I sit on a cemetery hillside in the woods, I am closer to nature. It is a very peaceful, warm atmosphere. I begin to think about where I am going in life. My life revolves around sports, music, driving, but most importantly, family and friends. I am not a partying type of guy, and I think this will give me an edge over those who care more about partying than they care about being someone in life.

I see myself graduating from college and getting a good job. I plan to get married and live in a nice house on the West Coast. But, I have to think: "Will it be this easy?" "Will I live long enough to do these things?" I wonder what it's like to be dead, and if the world will come to an end in my lifetime. "How old will I be when I die?" "Will people care that I am gone?" These are some pretty scary, but important, things to think about, and I don't believe many people ask themselves these questions.

Overall, I think of myself as well liked. I try to treat people with respect and think most people treat me the same. I hope people think enough of me to say nice things about me after I die. I want to make a name for myself.

Looking back on this assignment, I believe that getting closer to nature makes me think about some things I might not think of in the world of my daily life. I hope that thinking about the future will help me accomplish what I want in life.

BRIGETTE LAMBERT

Wahama High School

Mysteries of life to be discovered
Success and wealth to be achieved
My soul covered by the mask
of someone it is not

To have hope for the future
To find peace of mind
To bring joy in my life and
Love in my heart

Let the spirit God blessed shine through
to listen to the voice within,
grasping a unique power
I find only in myself.

CHAD MARSH
Weir High School

A s I sit in this serene setting provided by God, my mind is clear and I am oblivious to the things outside of this place. I wonder why I never took the time to enjoy this beautiful spot. I think about the many aspects of my seemingly monotonous, listless life.

With my back against an oak tree, I look at the path that cuts in front of me and makes this place accessible. This trail is wide and easily traveled at first. However, it becomes overrun by thorns and blocked by fallen trees until it is nearly unrecognizable. My existence is like this path. Problems that I encounter are like the thorn bushes on the path. The obstacles that I must overcome are the fallen trees. Like the path ahead, I cannot see my future, for it is cluttered with the thickets and falling timbers of possibility.

In my field of view is a large, decaying tree stump. It is long dead, yet saplings grow out of it. My ancestors, too, are long dead, but their name is passed along by a small sapling – me. When this old elm is totally decomposed only I will remember it. After my life is over, I do not want to be a faded memory. I want to never be forgotten.

Lost in my thoughts, I fail to notice that I am being hit by falling acorns. These acorns are like the people in my life. Many take root and become towering trees; however, some fail to do so and are quickly removed from my scene. I wonder if an acorn will fall from the tree of my life that is right for me. That is to say, will I find the girl of my dreams?

So many things around me bring to mind forgotten memories, thoughts I never took time to ponder before, and feelings I never knew I had. Nature brings about a change in a person that can transform his or her life forever – a change that I have undergone today.

ANDREA MARTIN
Buffalo High School

My life is like this rock I'm sitting on. Just as a rock can be part of the building of a road or the construction of a pathway, I can do the same. I want to make something of my life and help those in need. I want to help build the road one takes to a good future. I want to lend a hand to one who needs a hand to hold. This rock and I each have a future of building, helping, and making people's lives easier.

44

ASHLEY MARTIN
Buffalo High School

L ike the caterpillar that becomes the butterfly, my life in the future will be based on the experiences and education that I am gathering today. Butterflies are peaceful creatures, and I want to make the world a peaceful place for my family, friends, and others. If I cannot achieve all of my goals, I will still try to be like the butterfly and help others, as well as myself.

PHIL MCCOY

Parkersburg South High School

I want to be happy most of all. When most people think of being an adult, they have visions of trudging off to work and never escaping the rat race. I don't want my life to be like that.

I want to graduate from college, get a job—maybe even one I don't despise—and live somewhere nice. I don't need to be rich, but would like enough to keep me secure.

If I have a family, I wouldn't mind two or three kids. The setting for this fairytale life is somewhere in the Carolinas, along the coast. No hurricanes, though. My family and I would live on the beach with a fantastic view of fishing boats every morning.

I'd have my own business and wouldn't have to arrive at work until around noon. I'd leave around 6 o'clock. When I went home, my wife would have something delicious prepared for dinner: Chili, for instance, my favorite food.

While the sun was setting, I'd go outside and pass a football with my son. Then I'd come in for the night and relax. I'd read a book, watch TV, or waste time on the computer. Finally, I'd crawl into bed and sleep.

If my future could be like that – even if just slightly – I can imagine myself being very happy. This vision of my future might keep me working hard to reach my goal of having a happy life.

MEGAN MCLANE

Buffalo High School

As I sit here, a bee buzzes around my head. I compare myself to this bee in that I don't bother people unless they bother me. Bees seem to be joyful too, and I usually maintain a consistently good mood.

Bees also seem to follow one another. Anytime I see a bee, I usually see a couple more right behind it. I used to think that I was like this leader bee, but now I realize I am a follower. Being a follower is not a terrible thing. In some situations, following is the best path to take.

I wonder what these bees are thinking as they swarm around the trashcan. Could there be one like me wondering if it should be in front eating what the others are eating? Maybe there is, but there is also a leader who will lead them to a better place.

TIMMY HARLESS

Van High School

Fall is Here

The Autumn leaves are falling
slowly through the sky.
Sweaters and jackets are calling.
Warm days, cool nights
Birds starting to take flight
 Winter is calling by and by.

Fall is here.
Darkness comes sooner.
Thanksgiving is near.
The stars hang around the moon.
Flowers go to sleep for winter
 To wake up when spring re-enters.

Football games on Fridays,
The end of a long week.
Thoughts of snow are sweet.
Squirrel hunting in the woods:
 The meat isn't very good.

Halloween is in the fall.
Pumpkins, ghosts, and trick-or-treat
Decorations in school halls,
Children after candy, going up the streets,
Going home with lots of sweets:
 Children love to trick-or-treat.

Leaves, crunching under shoes,
Blowing in the wind,
Going far in the upward blue,
On the ground they blend.
Jumping in and out of them for fun,
*   Going in to dinner when we're done.*

Going to school on a frosty morning,
My breath freezing in the air.
Bright stars in the sky without warning,
Like they have no care.
How they twinkle and shine,
*   No higher can they climb.*

Shorts, sandals, and t-shirts
Put up for next year,
Resting in a box
Next to my baseball gear.
Activities planned inside
*   Where warm air always hides.*

Fall is my mother's favorite season,
She loves the colored leaves;
I believe that is the reason.
Fall is the trees getting sleepy;
Winter is coming again.
*   Fun times with snow will soon begin.*

AARON MCMAHAN
Parkersburg South High School

Individually, we are leaves, flapping in the chaos of the wind. It will not be until we join together that we will be able to provide shade for future generations.

BRIAN MOZINGO

Weir High School

During my time in the woods, the question I thought most about was "Who am I?" Sitting on a rock, by a tree, I might have found the answer. I am an ordinary person. Just like this tree, I live my life every day. Like the tree, I need nourishment. Like the rock on which I sit, I am hard to break.

My life is all about my friends and my family. It's about good food and fun. It's about the peace and quiet one discovers when they are walking in the woods alone and all they can hear is their footsteps.

To those who came before me, I am a follower, a listener, and a student. To those still to come, I hope to be a role model, a friend, a big brother, a father, and an uncle.

In five years my life will just be getting started. In ten years I hope my life is set. I hope to have a steady routine and have my life planned out.

When I am gone, the tree and the rock will still be here. Yet I know the tree will die some day, and so will I.

RYAN MULLEN

Parkersburg South High School

Life is what one makes of it. Despite one's start in life, each has the opportunity to be fulfilled. Whether we decide to work hard or take it easy is what determines who we are to become. Each must find out for themselves what a fulfilling life is and what they should become.

Money and status are not the measures of success, but how one feels inside. A king might not like how he feels inside while a peasant might wake up happy every morning.

CARRIE MULLINS
Buffalo High School

In the world I live in, I compare myself to a bird. Some days I prefer to be the leader at the front of the V. Some days I want to be a follower and take it easy for a while.

Birds are usually surrounded by other birds. Like a bird, I don't like to be alone. I like to be surrounded by my loved ones, those I care about and who also feel as I do. When I see a flying V in the sky, I think of the freedom birds have. Where are they going? What are they going to become? Only the leader can determine these things and find the path to a new life.

To help make the world a better place, I want to do what I can to make everyone feel like a bird. I want the world to know who I am and that it is okay to be a follower. I want to point out to the world that, if problems or situations start to get you down, you should let those feelings soar smoothly through the air because things won't get better until you've taken the time to rest.

LAUREL NEACE
Buffalo High School

My life is like a dandelion's. Some people think I'm a weed and some people think I'm a flower. Some people cut me down, some people help me grow and care for me. I think life is about getting cut down and having to grow back.

In the fall, my seeds will go in all directions, to other's lives. Some people will not accept my seed. Some will take it and let it grow in their lives.

Others may think me a weed, but I know I'm a flower.

CANA OLENICK

Weir High School

The leaves have changed color again. The weather is cooler and the days are darker. It's hard to believe that the leaves were green and the days were longer two weeks ago. Sitting here, I'm reminded of the different stages of life. These are the trees I once hid behind and under playing house as a child. This was the only world that mattered to me. I feel like it's gone. I'll never have the chance to play hide 'n seek until nightfall again. Why does life have to get so difficult? Why can't things stay simple? Why did my fun have to go by so quickly?

When I was little I wished to be a teenager. I thought "Things will change, it'll be great." Well, things did change. It seems like I wished away all my good years. Now I'm like the changing seasons. More red, orange, yellow and brown leaves will fall soon bringing me closer to next summer, my last summer here. Then I'll be off to a new, unexplored world. This is what I know: these surroundings, these people, these memories. I'm afraid I'll forget them. What if I do? What if the world changes *me*?

Each day is like a fallen leaf, destined to wither away. What if my memories wither away? I don't want the season to change.

JASMINE PENDERGRAST
Weir High School

As I lie in my front yard I look up at a tree and all of the branches that sprout from its trunk. Each branch is of a different size and represents the many obligations and responsibilities I have in my life. So much is expected of me. I am expected to get good grades, perform well in basketball, spend time with family, hang out with friends, and perform duties for the clubs to which I belong. But what about the shortest branch on the tree: me. When will I ever have time for myself?

I always seem to be stressed and fighting an uphill battle. Nothing ever seems to be good enough. Yet, when I do make mistakes, I try to make the best of the situation.

I see all different colors of leaves on the tree. I am like this, in that I show my true colors. I don't try to hide anything. I try to be honest with others and myself.

I agree with Anne Morrow Lindburgh when she says that Americans are always in a rush toward the future. We seem to seldom take the time to enjoy the simple things in the present. I am like this. I can't wait until I can go to college because it will be a different atmosphere. However, I have some fears about leaving.

The wind blows a leaf into the air and I am reminded of myself when I am happy and successful; as the saying goes: "What goes up, must come down." The falling leaf is like a sad point or failure in my life. No one wants to fail, but the more I think about it, failures are lessons I can learn from. Still, it's hard to go through these times. I know I am strong, but wonder if I'm strong enough to go through the difficult times by myself, once I leave home and the security of family and friends. I'm a little scared, but even more excited.

At this age, I have many questions and few answers. I know the only way to find the answers I need is to live my life. I want to make my dreams come true and make a difference. I want to be a positive role model who impresses upon kids the importance of being a leader.

Each tree has different colored leaves. Every leaf takes a different path to the ground, and no two of them land in the same spot. This is similar to America's "melting pot." Both are like the different kinds of people who come together to become one body. This reminds me that truly accepting diversity is the key to a better future.

JOANIE RAYNES
Buffalo High School

Sometimes I feel like a baby bird that has not yet learned to fly. Even though I have a family, I feel like no one's there to help me out of that tree. I feel like I'm stuck in the tree with no one to help me down.

Other times I feel like a blade of grass that gets cut down every time it starts growing. It's like they think I don't need to grow or be successful, but one day I will show them what I can be. I can be whatever I want to be.

COURTNEY SALTER

Weir High School

Who am I? I am an intelligent and beautiful human being who is not afraid to stand up for my beliefs and myself. I used to think that race defined a person, but I now find that it influences only part of your life. This confuses me because I am multiracial. But it is partly because of my internationally mixed background that some of my beliefs have been formed. I do not believe in prejudice. I try to like everyone for who they are and not what they look like or how they dress or any other invalid reason. I don't see things in black and white, but in many different colors. I wonder why more people aren't happy with how they look.

I am unsure what my life is all about, but I think that God has sent each of us here to fulfill a certain task. I don't know what my purpose is yet, but I do know that, whatever it is, I will do my best and hope to accomplish it.

I don't know where I am in relation to my ancestors, but the question reminded me of a story my great grandmother used to tell me. It was the story of her grandfather, who had been a slave. He had dreamed and fantasized of his children and their children being free. My great grandmother would tell me how he would hope for them to be able to walk down the street unashamed of who they were. Maybe I am the result of that dream. I am free. I can make decisions for myself. I can go places without worrying about being called insulting names. I walk down the street proud of who I am and where I came from, and I will tell this story to my children and my children's children, and they will tell their children, so that my great, great grandfather's dream will not be forgotten.

I often wonder what my life will be like in the future. In five years I will still be in college, studying fashion design and merchandising. Ten years from now I hope to be on my way to becoming someone who will change another person's life for the better. But what if I fail? What if I become one of those people who have to ask the question: "What if…?" That is why I try so hard now, so I don't end up like one of those "What if…?" people.

What possible contributions could I make? I might find a cure for AIDS; I might help orphans find good homes, or help battered wives and children feel like they are important. There are many contributions I could make. Ideally, I will.

Though I've written about a lot of things, I have probably neglected the most important thing: Where I went to spend my hour and what it brings to mind. I went to the playground in my neighborhood and sat in a little hut surrounded by brightly colored trees and rusted playground equipment. When I first sat down, I thought: "How could this remind me of something?" After I had written the preceding words I saw the place in a new light. I noticed that my surroundings reminded me of Nan, my grandmother. This hut has been here for as long as I can remember. It has survived the harshest weather. I usually come here when I am overwhelmed by life. In many ways, this hut is like Nana. She has been with me as long as I can remember. She has survived the hardest obstacles in life. Like this hut, I know that I can go to her when I am overwhelmed. As I look at the brightly colored fall leaves, I see Nana's personality. The rusted swing-set, which has worn through the years due to changes in weather and playful children, reminds me of Nana because she has aged through the years due to illness and active grandchildren.

Unfortunately, I do not see myself in any of these surroundings. Perhaps one day, when I am older and wiser, I will see a reflection of myself in this beautiful scenery.

✦

MARK SHOMSKY
Weir High School

As I sit in nature I look around and realize I'm just a tiny speck in this big, beautiful world. I notice a tree's great mass and strength as it reaches toward Heaven supported solely by a few roots in the ground. I realize the tree doesn't have to think about all of life's problems. All it does is live and spread its beauty over the earth. I wonder why I'm here and what my purpose is on this planet. I don't seem to have a clue why I'm here or what my life is going to be like ten years from now. Will I be someone important people can learn from or a person who doesn't have what it takes to teach others?

I am lying back watching the wind blow leaves off of trees

when a plastic bag flies by and reminds me that litter could kill our planet. I get up for about 15 minutes and collect other trash, thinking of the possible effects of that one bag. What if an animal thought it was edible, or crawled into it and suffocated? Littering has to be stopped or future generations might suffer from its horrible effects – even see their world overcome.

RACHEL THOMAS

Parkersburg South High School

Dreaming is my sanctuary. It is the one state where I know I can always find bliss. It is the state where no harm can come to me.

ADRIENNE TOWNSEND

Parkersburg South High School

I think life is what one makes it, and that we should each be thankful for what we have and what we can acquire. We should also try to find the reason we are each put on this earth. For myself, I believe that if someone thought I should be here, there must be a good reason for it. I want to be one with my surroundings and not take them for granted. The only thing I need is a good family so I can love and be loved back. Many people don't have that.

I believe that every person has some kind of effect on the world. As I grow, I hope to leave a positive effect on the world. I know that if I do what makes those around me and myself happy, I will have lived a good life.

BRYCE TRUSHEL
Weir High School

I sit in the serenity of nature, watching creatures duck in and out of their tiny homes in the ground and trees. These animals, full of life, scamper to prepare themselves for the coming winter. They are readying themselves to struggle and endure the cold and lack of sufficient food, not knowing if they have properly arranged for their survival. This seems to mimic my life, as I constantly prepare for what may come. I never know if what I have done will take me where I want to go. Like these animals, I can only hope that I will prosper and survive the obstacles that lie ahead.

I watch for more animals, and notice a doe and her two young fawns. She watches over her offspring, scanning for any impending danger. A slight crack of a twig warns of potential danger, and she bounds away with her offspring in pursuit. This makes me think of how my own parents have worked to make my life the best that it can be. My father, working day after day, and my mother raising me from a child. I hope that I can one day provide support for my family the way my parents have for me. I would also like to instill in my children the morals my parents instilled in me.

In a few years, I hope to be in college, majoring in an engineering field. I aspire to graduate with a Masters degree, or possibly even a Ph.D. I plan to marry and have children. From that point, I hope to take life as it comes and handle problems as they occur. I want to draw upon my experience to determine the best possible actions.

What contributions I will make is impossible to know. I would like to say that I will send a man to Mars or find a cure for cancer, but I will only know when the time comes. I must live my life each day. I must always remember where I came from since I will never truly know where I am going. I must always remember who and what helped me reach my goals; only then will I be successful in life.

DAVE WARWICK
Weir High School

O n Saturday, 14 October 2000, something occurred that changed my outlook on life. My friends and I were driving around King's Creek and stopped by Chad Galownia's house to get a football. I went to get back in the car with David James DeFelice and Brett Allen, who I'd been riding with all day, but something stopped me. I had left my shirt in Chad's car and rode with him so I could put it back on. David James and Brett wrecked at the bottom of Lick Run Hill. Chad and I found Brett and he told us what had happened. We went to the scene and saw the car. It had been totaled, landing upside-down in a ditch.

I looked at the back seat, where I had been riding, and saw how the roof of the car had been flattened. It occurred to me that I could have died that day. Had I not gone back to Chad's car to get my shirt, I would have been riding in the back seat with my seatbelt off as I had been doing all day. It's stunning to think that a small decision like choosing to put my shirt back on possibly saved my life.

Perhaps I'm here to accomplish something that I haven't done yet. Maybe I have someone watching out for me above. All three of us could have been permanently maimed or killed, but we weren't. Although we were very good friends before this, we're even closer now.

That day we were treating the wreck like a big joke, but today, it really means something to us. I think about how we complain about our lives. I now know that's not the way to think. Now I know I should think: "At least I'm alive." Little things don't seem to bother me much today. Also, I have discovered something new about me: I'm not an athlete; I'm an actor. Because of the accident, I decided to care less about what other people think and take parts in plays. In the theater, I have found not only new friends, but new people who are as much a family as my old friends are to me. That, I now realize, is who I am: those that matter to me and those who are a part of me. I don't know how the future will be or what it will bring, but I do know that those people will always be a major part of my life.

ANDREW COCHRAN
Buffalo High School

My life is like a pebble: small, well rounded, and smooth.
I don't do many things, but I'm willing to try a few.
I want to learn more about myself
by thinking, reading, and writing.

Maybe when I grow up, I'll grow myself a garden.
Maybe when I grow up, I'll go into dentistry
so all of my patients can have pretty teeth.
As I look back on my life thus far, I have to say that I've had fun,
but for now I have to go, the dismissal bell has rung.

RONDA WILSON
Weir High School

I sit here thinking about my life and what may become of it. I don't feel like I'm going anywhere. As I look around, I see bugs going through their lives with seemingly nothing in their way. I hear birds singing the song of praise for making it another day. "What is my life?" "Why am I here?" "What will I become?" "On what morning will I wake to see what I wanted the night before?"

Sitting here opens my mind to many things. Birds' lives seem so short, but they seem to fulfill their destinies. They do what they have to do to ensure there will be another generation. Humans seem to try to make our lives how we want them and not think about what will happen in the future to our children and our selves.

I think of these things and realize I don't know who I am. I could say I am a 16-year-old girl trying to make something of my life and hoping I don't mess it up. I wish I had it easy, but understand that God will not give me anything I can't handle.

I'd like to know what my life is all about. Why did God put me here? I think it's a journey to return to Him. I think he put us here to see who would have the passion inside to be strong enough to return to Him.

I think there were more strong and passionate people in the past than there are now. Today, it seems that people care more about themselves, and less about others.

In five years I hope to be in college furthering my education. In ten years I hope to be an educated and respected pediatrician. I hope that I can contribute to many people's lives and help them. I strive to one day touch people's lives like Martin Luther King, John F. Kennedy, and Abraham Lincoln. My goal is to die with a smile on my face and peace in my heart. I know that if I could be filled with comfort and respect, I could die with no fear.

My one, true wish is that I will return to the Heavenly Father and He will say to me: "Ronda, my daughter, I love you and have missed you." Then I will know that my spirit and my life were complete.

Sitting here looking at all God created, it makes me proud that He allowed me to be here and witness such wonders. Even though the assignment instructs me to be alone, the wind lets me know He is with me every time it blows. Even though I don't consider myself a "nature person," I know that nature is a part of me. I would like to stay out here and watch everything that happens, but I realize I can't because I have a life to lead. I hope I can do it with grace and dignity.

LYNSEY WISEMAN
Parkersburg South High School

I don't think I will ever truly understand myself. I don't think anyone ever does. People are so complicated. We have so many thoughts and emotions all the time, there's no way to understand them all. I wonder why I get so excited about some things, and so depressed about others. I wonder why some things make certain people like me and not others. They say that nobody knows you as well as you know yourself, but I doubt that at times. I can't think of anyone who knows me really well, but I seem to be such a stranger to myself that there must be someone who knows me better than I do.

Sometimes I wish I did understand myself completely, but I realize that if I did know everything about myself, life wouldn't be as interesting and exciting. We wouldn't have the exciting and enjoyable times that we have when we find out something new about ourselves. I guess I can say that my life is better the way it is, not totally understanding myself and learning more about the person I am every day.

ZACH YOKLIC

Weir High School

The chirping of crickets surrounds me. I can't get close because every time I try, they stop. No sunlight is reaching me now; the clouds are too thick. The wind is making odd sounds. I hear the chattering birds. Nearby are three deer beds. The oblong shapes are close together. Are they for a family? Wow! Four deer just ran across the meadow! They are silent until they get to the trees, and then crash noisily into the forest. The pine trees seem so stalwart among their needles.

What am I in this world? I seem so out of place in this simple environment. I doubt rabbits worry about their SAT scores, or if a beech thinks about its future. I bet that others don't wonder if time is linear, or spend hours contemplating their world. Am I going to end up adrift without knowing what I'm trying to accomplish? Am I going to try to be someone I'm not? I love doing many things because I WANT to do them. I'm not sure I'll want to do those things for pay. Would they hold the same magic? Does the fact that my intelligence opens many paths to me make my choice harder?

The leaves of the tree I am leaning upon seem to drink up the sun's light. This makes me think of the many autumns I have watched from my window. I've talked to my parents about my ancestors, and they told me that those people weren't like me. Would my ancestors understand me at all? Why am I so different? Will everyone to come in my family be like me? I hope not. That would be boring.

ERICA ZABLACKAS
Weir High School

The falling leaves remind me of graceful ballerinas twirling through the air. Humans are sometimes like leaves. Life is sometimes like that downward spiral, not ending until one hits the bottom. Then we realize that we're not the only leaf on the ground, and that there are people with troubles just like us. Everyone ends up like a leaf on the ground at one time or another. Then, just like leaves in the spring, we grow and become beautiful again. Whenever life is at its worst, a person begins to grow, and life eventually improves.

If I were to compare my life now to a leaf, it would be late spring. I'm beginning to know who I really am now, and I'm happy I'm not like everybody else. I try to always be myself, but it's not that easy. I don't mind that most people don't share my interests. I don't mind silence, and I enjoy being alone to daydream.

I don't know too much about those who came before me, but I would like to know more about my roots and what my ancestor's lives were like. I hope future generations will be able to trace their ancestry better than we can.

In five years I hope to be in my senior year of college. I imagine it will be stressful as I draw nearer to graduating and living on my own for the first time. I think it will be exciting being on my own, but also scary since I might not have as much security as I had growing up. My life in ten years is even more difficult to predict, but I hope I will have established myself in a teaching career. If so, I will encourage my students to take pride in being different, so that they might become like leaves in the spring, growing into all different shapes, sizes, and colors, scattered everywhere, and achieving their greatest potential.

PUBLISHERS PLACE, INC.

I t started in a sandwich shop, Schlotszky's on 4th avenue in downtown Huntington. A handful of "creative types" talking about renting office space together and splitting the cost of utilities, copier, Internet access and telephone service. How could they get help paying for the office while they worked on their separate publishing projects—a consultancy in book development, a small publishing enterprise, a budding magazine and one member looking for storage space for the archives of West Virginia Writers, Inc.?

Why not, someone said, put out an annual calendar? Why not gather up some of the best examples of West Virginia photographers as the headshots and cameo shots?

What about text? Why not try excerpts of poetry? After all, unknown to most of the nation, West Virginia had some of the best poets and writers in America.

And so the adventure was launched—Publishers Place. Within eighteen months the organization had won its 501-c-3 nonprofit status from very tough Internal Revenue Service reviewers, had published its first *Pride in West Virginia* calendar (1998) and had offices down the street from Schlotszky's, next to the Keith Albee Theater on the second floor streetside of the Huntington Arcade.

The shakeout from the original five people involved in the creation of Publishers Place, Inc., left John Patrick Grace, a book editor, and Mark Phillips, a graphic designer, as co-directors. The others continued in a supporting role—Doug Imbrogno, feature editor of *The Charleston Gazette*, Lynda Holup, now a marketing executive with the Marshall University School of Medicine, and Kirk Judd, a quality engineer at

Special Metals, Inc., in Huntington and a celebrated performance poet and writing workshop leader.

Five years and counting later, Publishers Place, Inc., has issued five successive calendars, two collections of writing out of solitude by West Virginia high-school students (*River Fog Rising* and *Light that Splits the Dark*), and the astonishing anthology, *Wild Sweet Notes: Fifty Years of West Virginia Poetry (1950-1999)*. The 436-page volume was, from what could be determined, the best-selling book in the state in autumn of 2000, and has already gone into its third printing. It also was short listed for the prestigious American Poetry Anthology Award.

What's ahead? Publishers Place continues to compile a database of all professionals and amateurs involved in the publishing arts in West Virginia, building toward an annual get-together for cross fertilization and synergy. There is the prospect of a second poetry anthology—*Wild Sweet Notes II*— a coffeetable volume of portfolios from the state's best photographers and possibly a children's book on growing up in West Virginia. Stay tuned for more exciting developments as we enter our second five years!

> **Mission Statement**—*to encourage, promote and elevate the quality of the publishing arts in West Virginia for citizens of all ages.*

82

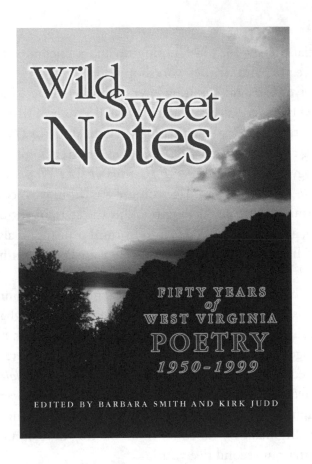

134 poets • 432 pages
Illustrated • Indexed
Hardcover • ISBN 0-9676051-0-5 • $29.95
Softbound • ISBN 0-9676051-1-3 • $19.95
Special Limited Edition Also Available

Wild Sweet Notes: Fifty Years of West Virginia Poetry (1950-1999), edited by Barbara Smith and Kirk Judd, was three years in the making and brought together 134 West Virginia poets working in the second half of the 20th century.

With insights into Japanese flower gardening and hog butchering, into mother-daughter relations and horse trading, in verse that is wistful or bright or drenched in rural beauty, *Wild Sweet Notes: Fifty Years of West Virginia Poetry* surprises and delights. . . . This varied collection of remarkably high poetic quality will enchant readers throughout the English-speaking world.

83

Precise observation, a careful ear, a devotion to detail. . . . Lucid and engaging. Voices, lore, and landscape. . . resound distinctively.
— *ForeWord Magazine*, September 2000

Over the mountains, throughout the land, the stars are out. They are West Virginia poets brought together for the first time, shining as never before. Clear and bright, enough light to read by. This is what we've been waiting for.
— *Grace Cavalieri*, Producer
"The Poet and the Poem" on National Public Radio (USA)

An ode to West Virginia. . . . A wealth of knowledge, compassion, and inspiration.
— Charleston [WV] *Sunday Gazette-Mail*